70/1558L

Jazz Music for Christmas

Lani Smith

Carol Duets for One Piano - Four Hands

Editor: David Sarandon
Music Engraving: Jeanette Dotson
Cover Design: Jeff Richards

ISBN: 978-0-89328-851-8

Lorenz Publishing Company Box 802 · Dayton, Ohio 45401
www.lorenz.com

Good King Wenceslas

Lani Smith
Based on a traditional English melody

Duration: 1:45

JD

Go, Tell It on the Mountain

Lani Smith
Based on a traditional melody

Duration: 2:15

What Child Is This?

Lani Smith
Tune: **GREENSLEEVES**
a traditional English melody

Duration: 1:55

Away in a Manger

Lani Smith
Based on a traditional American melody
and quoting CRADLE SONG *by Johannes Brahms*

Duration: 1:40

JD

The First Nowell

Lani Smith
Based on a traditional English melody

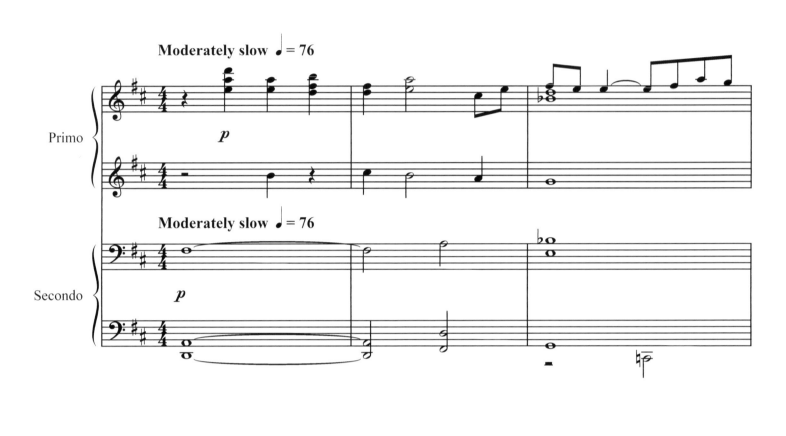

Duration: 3:10

www.lorenz.com

Silent Night

Lani Smith
Tune: **STILLE NACHT**
by Franz Gruber

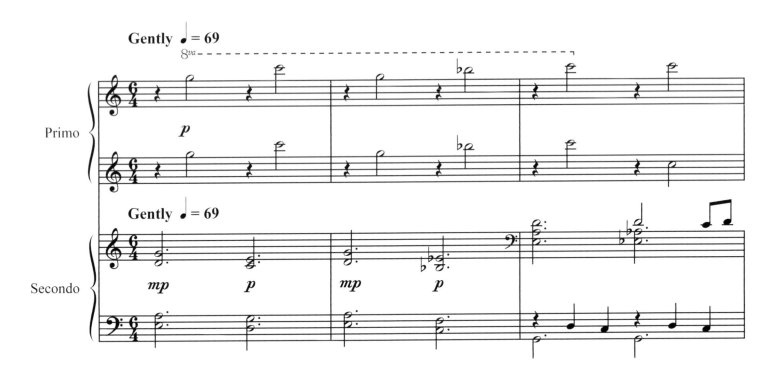

Duration: 2:45

JD

O Little Town of Bethlehem

Lani Smith
Tune: ST. LOUIS
by Lewis H. Redner

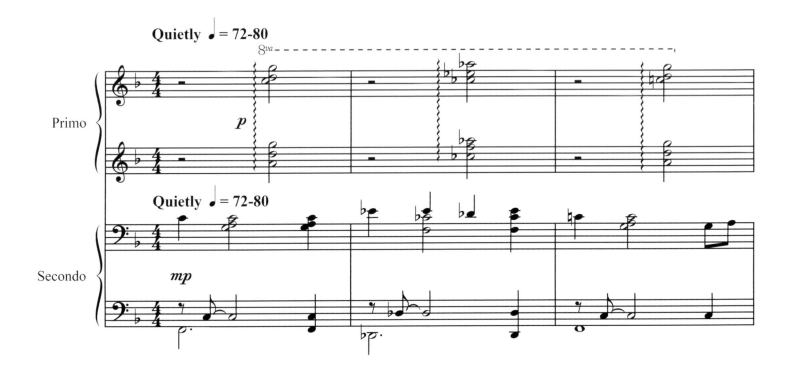

Duration: 2:00

JD

Angels We Have Heard on High

Lani Smith
Tune: **GLORIA**
a traditional French melody

Duration: 1:50

JD